Presented to:

....

By:

....

Date:

....

A HELEN STEINER RICE ® Product

© 2012 by Barbour Publishing, Inc.

All poems © Helen Steiner Rice Foundation Fund, LLC, a wholly owned subsidiary of Cincinnati Museum Center. All rights reserved. Published under license from the Helen Steiner Rice Foundation Fund, LLC.

Written and compiled by Nanette Anderson and Elece Hollis in association with Snapdragon Group℠, Tulsa, OK.

Print ISBN 978-1-62029-167-2

eBook Editions:
Adobe Digital Edition (.epub) 978-1-62029-676-9
Kindle and MobiPocket Edition (.prc) 978-1-62029-675-2

Published by Barbour Publishing, Inc., P.O. Box 719, Uhrichsville, Ohio 44683, www.barbourbooks.com

Our mission is to publish and distribute inspirational products offering exceptional value and biblical encouragement to the masses.

 Member of the
Evangelical Christian
Publishers Association

Printed in China.

Meet God in the Morning

Poems for the Heart of Prayer

HELEN
STEINER
RICE

BARBOUR
PUBLISHING

Contents

Prayer

Listen to my voice
in the morning, LORD.
Each morning I bring
my requests to you
and wait expectantly.

PSALM 5:3 NLT

Are You Listening?

*I*magine a teenager sitting in the passenger seat of your car. You speak, but he doesn't respond. The iPod in his hand and the earbuds tell you he's fully involved in his music. You ask about his day, but he doesn't hear you. He knows you're there, even turns your way and smiles distractedly. But clearly he isn't listening.

Too often this is how we come to God in prayer. We know He's there, but we're too distracted by the business of life to have a conversation with Him. Instead we quickly tell Him what we need and get back to what we were doing.

God longs to speak with you, to help you navigate the world you live in. He wants to share His wisdom with you, give you counsel and direction. But you must choose to set aside the distractions and really listen to what He has to say.

Daily Prayers
Dissolve Your Cares

I meet God in the morning
   and go with Him through the day,
Then in the stillness of the night
   before sleep comes I pray
That God will just take over
   all the problems I couldn't solve,
And in the peacefulness of sleep
   my cares will all dissolve.
So when I open up my eyes
   to greet another day,
I'll find myself renewed in strength
   and there will open up a way
To meet what seemed impossible
   for me to solve alone,
And once again I'll be assured
   I am never on my own.

—HSR

God, Are You There?

I'm way down here—You're way up there
Are You sure You can hear
    my faint, faltering prayer?
For I'm so unsure of just how to pray—
To tell You the truth, God,
    I don't know what to say.
I just know I'm lonely and vaguely disturbed,
Bewildered and restless,
    confused and perturbed,
And they tell me that prayer
    helps to quiet the mind
And to unburden the heart,
    for in stillness we find
A newborn assurance that
    someone does care
And someone does answer
    each small, sincere prayer.

—HSR

Begin Each Day
by Kneeling to Pray

Start every day with a
"good morning" prayer
And God will bless
each thing you do
and keep you in His care. . .
And never, never sever
the spirit's silken strand
That our Father up in heaven
holds in His mighty hand.

—HSR

Honest Words

On any given day, you might hear prayers that are planned, rehearsed, and lovely, spoken in gilded voices using carefully chosen words. There is nothing wrong with a beautiful formal prayer in public, yet in your personal prayers, God wants fresh words, true words, and honest expressions. He wants you to speak from your heart.

This morning as you meet with God, try speaking to Him; as you would to a trusted friend. The God who created the universe isn't going to be impressed with your fancy words anyway. Spill out your needs to Him; ask Him to help you make a success of all you do. Then listen for His answer.

When He speaks, you won't hear Him with your physical ears. As you get quiet, His voice will resonate in your spirit deep down inside you. And His words will be simple and honest as well.

The First Thing
Every Morning and the
Last Thing Every Night

Were you too busy this morning
   to quietly stop and pray?
Did you hurry and drink your coffee
   then frantically rush away,
Consoling yourself by saying,
   God will always be there
Waiting to hear my petitions,
   ready to answer each prayer?
It's true that the great, generous Savior
   forgives our transgressions each day
And patiently waits for lost sheep
   who constantly seem to stray,

But moments of prayer once omitted
  in the busy rush of the day
Can never again be recaptured,
  for they silently slip away.
Strength is gained in the morning
  to endure the trials of the day
When we visit with God in person
  in a quiet and unhurried way,
For only through prayer that's unhurried
  can the needs of the day be met
And only prayers said at evening
  can we sleep without fears or regret.
For all of our errors and failures
  that we made in the course of the day
Are freely forgiven at nighttime
  when we kneel down and earnestly pray,
So seek the Lord in the morning
  and never forget Him at night,
For prayer is an unfailing blessing
  that makes every burden seem light.

—HSR

It's Me Again, God

Remember me, God?
  I come every day
Just to talk with You, Lord,
  and to learn how to pray.
You make me feel welcome,
  You reach out Your hand.
I need never explain,
  for You understand.
I come to You frightened
  and burdened with care,
So lonely and lost
  and so filled with despair,
And suddenly, Lord,
  I'm no longer afraid—
My burden is lighter
  and the dark shadows fade.
Oh, God, what a comfort
  to know that You care
And to know when I seek You,
  You will always be there.

—HSR

Let me hear what God
the Lord will speak,
for he will speak peace
to his people, to his faithful,
to those who turn to him
in their hearts.

PSALM 85:8 NRSV

Perfect Peace

What is peace? Is it the absence of turmoil, a magical day when everything seems to be going well? Does it consist only of calm and quiet and a fragile sense of security? Unfortunately, that's as close as most people come to experiencing peace. But for those who entrust their lives to God, there is a whole new dimension of peace.

This God type of peace isn't affected by circumstances. It is the result of a simple knowing that God can be trusted with the affairs of your life. This amazing peace isn't something you can take up at a moment's notice. You find it as you come before God morning after morning and spend time talking things over with Him.

You don't know what another day holds for you—none of us do. But you can know the peace that comes from putting your day, whatever it brings, in God's hands.

The Prayer of Peace

Our Father up in heaven,
  hear this fervent prayer—
May the people of all nations
  be united in Thy care...
For earth's peace and man's salvation
  can come only by Thy grace
And not through bombs and missiles
  and our quest for outer space...
For until all men recognize
  that the battle is the Lord's
And peace on earth cannot be won
  with strategy and swords,
We will go on vainly fighting
  as we have in ages past,
Finding only empty victories
  and a peace that cannot last...
But we've grown so rich and mighty
  and so arrogantly strong

We no longer ask in humbleness—
  God, show us where we're wrong.
We have come to trust completely
  in the power of manmade things,
Unmindful of God's mighty power
  and that He is King of kings.
We have turned our eyes away from Him
  to go our selfish way,
And money, power, and pleasure
  are the gods we serve today. . .
And the good green earth God gave us
  to peacefully enjoy
Through greed and fear and hatred
  we are seeking to destroy.
Oh Father up in heaven,
  stir and wake our sleeping souls,
Renew our faith and lift us up
  and give us higher goals,
And grant us heavenly guidance
  as war threatens us again—
For more than guided missiles,
  all the world needs guided men.

                                        —HSR

The Comfort and Sweetness of Peace

After the clouds, the sunshine,
After the winter, the spring,
After the shower, the rainbow—
For life is a changeable thing,
After the night, the morning
Bidding all darkness cease,
After life's cares and sorrows,
The comfort and sweetness of peace.

—HSR

World Peace

World peace—it's the wish of many a pageant winner, and recently, a famous athlete made it his last name. Have you ever wondered what it really means though? Are we talking about a world without war? Maybe a world without discord or trouble? Whatever it is, we are unlikely to experience it in this life.

What we can experience is inner peace. We can overcome our own inner turmoil and discord by placing our lives in God's hands. We can stop the fretting and worrying by trusting in His goodness and making the changes He says are necessary.

You can have peace this morning—real peace— in the midst of a world filled with warfare and tragedy. It comes from just one source, God Himself. It is His promise when you walk with Him and purposefully let Him direct your thoughts and your actions.

Peace Begins in the Home
and in the Heart

Peace is not something you fight for
    with bombs and missiles that kill—
Peace is attained in the silence that comes
    when the heart stands still. . .
For hearts that are restless and warlike
    with longings that never cease
Can never contribute ideas
    that bring the world nearer to peace. . .
For as dew never falls on a morning
    that follows a dark, stormy night,
The peace and grace of our Father
    fall not on a soul in flight. . .
So if we seek peace for all people,
    there is but one place to begin,
And the armament race will not win it,
    for the fortress of peace is within.

—HSR

A Prayer for Peace

Give us strength and courage
    to be honorable and true
And to place our trust implicitly
    in unseen things and You. . .
And keep us kind and humble
    and fill our hearts with love,
Which in this selfish, greedy world
    man has so little of.
Forgive us our transgressions
    and help us find the way
To a better world for everyone
    where man walks in peace each day.

—HSR

Peace

If we could just lift up our hearts
Like flowers to the sun
And trust His Easter promise
And pray, "Thy will be done,"
We'd find the peace we're seeking,
The kind no man can give—
The peace that comes from knowing
He died so we might live!

—HSR

Thankfulness

Give thanks to him
and praise his name.
For the LORD is good.

PSALM 100:4-5 NLT

Tiny Treasures

*H*ave you ever noticed that a child can spend hours outdoors examining grass and sticks? Children are like that. They notice the little things—a feather lying in the grass, a shell poking up out of the sand, an interesting pebble in the driveway. They appreciate the beauty and uniqueness of the world around them. But it seems like we grown-ups often get too busy with life to notice the beauty and design in everyday things.

How long has it been since you took the time to look around you—really look? God has filled our world with so much beauty, so much to be grateful for. And it pleases Him when we slow down and see His treasures—the great, the small, and the tiny.

This morning as you prepare for your day, thank God for His creative genius demonstrated all around you. Tell Him how much you appreciate all He's done.

Thank You, God, for Everything

Thank You, God, for everything—
   the big things and the small—
For every good gift comes from God,
   the Giver of them all,
And all too often we accept
   without any thanks or praise
The gifts God sends as blessings
   each day in many ways.
And so at this time we offer up a prayer
To thank You, God, for giving us
   a lot more than our share.
First, thank You for the little things
   that often come our way—
The things we take for granted
   and don't mention when we pray—

The unexpected courtesy,
  the thoughtful, kindly deed,
A hand reached out to help us
  in the time of sudden need.
Oh make us more aware, dear God,
  of little daily graces
That come to us with sweet surprise
  from never-dreamed-of places.
Then thank You for the miracles
  we are much too blind to see,
and give us new awareness of
  our many gifts from Thee.
And help us to remember that
  the key to life and living
Is to make each prayer a prayer of thanks
  and each day a day of thanksgiving.

                                        —HSR

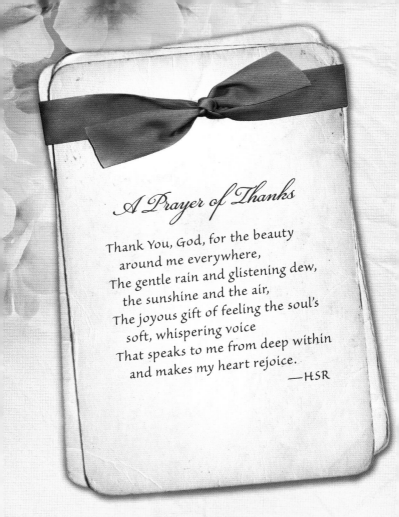

A Prayer of Thanks

Thank You, God, for the beauty
around me everywhere,
The gentle rain and glistening dew,
the sunshine and the air,
The joyous gift of feeling the soul's
soft, whispering voice
That speaks to me from deep within
and makes my heart rejoice.

—HSR

Saying Thanks

Doesn't it make you feel good when you receive a thank-you for all the things you do? Maybe it's a child thanking you for a good meal or help with homework. Or it might be a neighbor who thanks you for helping out during a difficult time. It could even be a letter from a charity thanking you for your donation. Yes, thankful words are always welcome.

As you come before God this morning, thank Him for all He's done for you, all the blessings He has so generously poured out on your life. Thankfulness in your heart is a good thing, but putting that thankfulness into words is even better.

Thankfulness is pleasing to God. You can be sure of that. So let your thankful words flow freely and bless the heart of God! Then get ready to receive God's blessing in return.

A Thankful Heart

Take nothing for granted, for whenever you do,
The joy of enjoying is lessened for you.
For we rob our own lives
   much more than we know
When we fail to respond or in any way show
Our thanks for the blessings
   that daily are ours—
The warmth of the sun, the fragrance of flowers,
The beauty of twilight, the freshness of dawn,
The coolness of dew on a green velvet lawn,

The kind little deeds so thoughtfully done,
The favors of friends and the love that someone
Unselfishly gives us in a myriad of ways,
Expecting no payment and no words of praise.
Oh, great is our loss when we no longer find
A thankful response to things of this kind.
For the joy of enjoying and the fullness of living
Are found in the heart that is
    filled with thanksgiving.

—HSR

Things to Be Thankful For

The good, green earth beneath our feet,
The air we breathe, the food we eat,
Some work to do, a goal to win,
A hidden longing deep within
That spurs us on to bigger things
And helps us meet what each day brings—
All these things and many more
Are things we should be thankful for. . .
And most of all, our thankful prayers
Should rise to God because He cares.

—HSR

Renewal

Outwardly we are wasting away,
yet inwardly we are being
renewed day by day.

2 CORINTHIANS 4:16 NIV

Cotton Soil

*D*id you know that growing cotton robs the land of minerals and nutrients? In years past, when the soil became depleted, the cotton grower simply moved on. But things are different now. Farmers have learned to renew the soil by planting legumes, adding fertilizers, and allowing the land to rest.

You may think that the soil of your heart is all used up, depleted, good for nothing. If so, don't despair. There are ways to make it productive again. As you meet with God this morning, ask Him to help you turn over the soil by confessing your wrongs and receiving God's forgiveness. Open your Bible and let the fresh water of God's Word flow across your dried-up places. Say yes to God's presence in your life, allowing it to rejuvenate the soil with precious spiritual nutrients. Soon you will be growing good crops again.

Renewal

When life has lost its luster
 and it's filled with dull routine,
When you long to run away from it,
 seeking pastures new and green,
Remember, no one runs away from life
 without finding when they do
That you can't escape the thoughts you think
 that are pressing down on you—
For though the scenery may be different,
 it's the same old heart and mind
And the same old restless longings that
 you tried to leave behind. . .
So when your heart is heavy
 and your day is dull with care,
Instead of trying to escape,
 why not withdraw in prayer?

For in prayer there is renewal
    of the spirit, mind, and heart,
For everything is lifted up
    in which God has a part—
For when we go to God in prayer,
    our thoughts are rearranged,
So even though our problems
    have not been solved or changed,
Somehow the good Lord gives us
    the power to understand
That He who holds tomorrow
    is the One who holds our hands.

                                        —HSR

After the Winter God Sends the Spring

Springtime is a season of
  hope and joy and cheer—
There's beauty all around us
  to see and touch and hear. . .
So no matter how downhearted
  and discouraged we may be,
New hope is born when we behold
  leaves budding on a tree
Or when we see a timid flower
  push through the frozen sod
And open wide in glad surprise
  its petaled eyes to God. . .
For this is just God saying,
  "Lift up your eyes to Me,
And the bleakness of your spirit,
  like the budding springtime tree,
Will lose its wintry darkness
  and your heavy heart will sing."
For God never sends the winter
  without the joy of spring.

—HSR

Refresh and Renew

*E*very day we spend time maintaining those things that help us live our lives. We change the oil in the car, prune back the roses, give the floors a good cleaning. Dust and polish. By doing these things, we renew the value and usefulness of our possessions.

It is also important to maintain, refresh, and renew other less obvious aspects of our lives. For example, we may need to spend time with a spouse or child in order to maintain or renew a vital relationship. We may need to sort out our hurt feelings and misunderstandings, or repair a rift in a friendship. We may need to check in with a neighbor or close friend.

What a tragedy it would be to realize that you have carefully maintained your possessions while neglecting what really matters. Ask God, this morning, what needs to be done. He'll help you see who and what needs your attention.

Today's Joy Was Born of Yesterday's Sorrow

Who said the darkness of the night
   would never turn to day?
Who said the winter's bleakness
   would never pass away?
Who said the fog would never lift
   and let the sunshine through?
Who said the skies, now overcast,
   would nevermore be blue?
Why should we ever entertain these thoughts
   so dark and grim

And let the brightness of our minds
  grow cynical and dim
When we know beyond all questioning
  that winter turns to spring
And on the notes of sorrow
  new songs are made to sing?
For on one sheds a teardrop
  or suffers loss in vain,
For God is always there to turn
  our losses into gain. . .
And every burden borne today
  and every present sorrow
Are but God's happy harbingers
  of a joyous, bright tomorrow.

—HSR

Good Morning, God

You are ushering in another day,
  untouched and freshly new,
So here I am to ask You, God,
  if You'll renew me, too. . .
Forgive the many errors
  that I made yesterday
And let me try again, dear God,
  to walk closer in Thy way. . .
But, Father, I am well aware
  I can't make it on my own,
So take my hand and hold it tight
  for I can't walk alone.

—HSR

Quietness

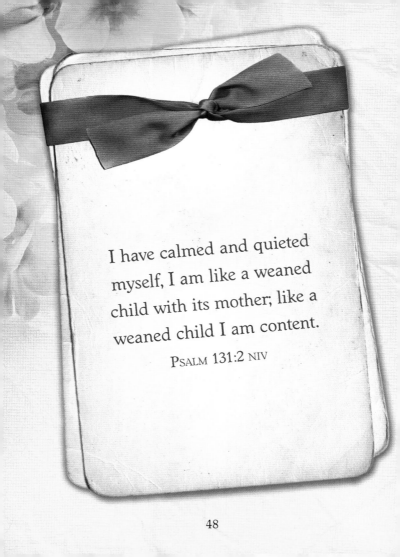

I have calmed and quieted myself, I am like a weaned child with its mother; like a weaned child I am content.

PSALM 131:2 NIV

Help Me!

The car swerves, careens off the shoulder of the highway, and crashes through a fenced pasture before shuddering to a stop. The driver sits in stunned silence for a few moments and then picks up the phone and calls for help. Hearing that someone is on the way, the driver stops struggling and waits quietly for help to come.

This is how we have learned to deal with physical emergencies. But what about those crises that are not so straightforward, the ones that wound our hearts and destroy our confidence? In those situations, can we call out to God and wait quietly for His help to arrive? We can do that if we know, like the rescue personnel, He's always standing by, watching out for us, and waiting for us to call for help.

Call on God, and then wait quietly for Him. When you need Him, He is always there to help.

The Peace of Meditation

So we may know God better
   and feel His quiet power,
Let us daily keep in silence a meditation hour. . .
For to understand God's greatness
   and to use His gifts each day,
The soul must learn to meet Him
   in a meditative way. . .
For our Father tells His children
   that if they would know His will
They must seek Him in the silence
   when all is calm and still. . .
For nature's great forces are found in quiet things
Like softly falling snowflakes
   drifting down on angels' wings
Or petals dropping soundlessly
   from a lovely full-blown rose,

So God comes closest to us
    when our souls are in repose...
So let us plan with prayerful care
    to always allocate
A certain portion of each day
    to be still and meditate...
For when everything is quiet
    and we're lost in meditation,
Our souls are then preparing
    for a deeper dedication
That will make it wholly possible
    to quietly endure
The violent world around us,
    for in God we are secure.

—HSR

Listen in the Quietness

To try to run away from life is impossible to do,
For no matter where you chance to go,
   your troubles will follow you—
For though the scenery is different,
   when you look deep inside you'll find
The same deep, restless longings
   that you thought you left behind...
So when life becomes a problem
   much too great for us to bear,
Instead of trying to escape,
   let us withdraw in prayer—
For withdrawal means renewal
   if we withdraw to pray
And listen in the quietness
   to hear what God will say.

—HSR

A Quiet Place

There aren't many places on earth where you can experience absolute silence. On a farm, you might hear the rustling of leaves against a fence; the sounds of animals, big and small, calling out to one another; and birds filling the air with music and chatter. At home in the city, you have the sounds of traffic and neighbors working in the yard. Fortunately, quieting your heart before God doesn't always mean eliminating all the sounds of life.

The quiet you find in God's presence might include the splashing of water as you wash dishes, the sound of the spade rubbing against the dirt and stone as you work in the garden, the waves crashing as you sit on the beach. God's quiet comes in the middle of your noisy life. Wherever you are this morning, quiet your heart, and reach out to God.

Learn to Rest So Your Life Will Be Blessed

We all need short vacations
    in life's fast and maddening race—
An interlude of quietness
    from the constant, jet-age pace,
So when your day is pressure-packed
    and your hours are all too few
Just close your eyes and meditate
    and let God talk to you. . .
For when we keep on pushing,
    we're not following in God's way—
We are foolish, selfish robots
    mechanized to fill each day
With unimportant trivia
    that makes life more complex
And gives us greater problems
    to irritate and vex.

So when your nervous network
    becomes a tangled mess,
Just close your eyes in silent prayer
    and ask the Lord to bless
Each thought that you are thinking,
    each decision you must make,
As well as every word you speak
    and every step you take—
For only by the grace of God
    can you gain self-control,
And only meditative thoughts
    can restore your peace and soul.

—HSR

Inspiration! Meditation!
Dedication!

Brighten your day
And lighten your way
And lessen your cares
With daily prayers.
Quiet your mind
And leave tension behind
And find inspiration
In hushed meditation.

—HSR

Praise be to the God and
Father of our Lord Jesus Christ,
who has blessed us in the
heavenly realms with every
spiritual blessing in Christ.

EPHESIANS 1:3 NIV

Handing Out Blessings

At the grocery store, one of the checkers is handing out blessings. Her bright smile and cheery greeting would be enough, but she adds to that by saying, "Have a blessed day," as she hands customers their receipts. Imagine what that simple gesture means to those who are discouraged and struggling with difficult circumstances in their lives.

Like that checker, you can bless others with simple words in passing, with your smile, a friendly wave, a positive attitude, a cheerful countenance. You can make a difference in every life you touch.

Think about this as you enter your time with God this morning. Ask Him to show you how to hand out blessings everywhere you go. The world around you will seem brighter, and without a doubt those blessings will come back to you. That's the way it is with God: the more you give to others, the more He lavishes His blessings on you.

Look on the Sunny Side

There are always two sides—
    the good and the bad,
The dark and the light, the sad and the glad. . .
But in looking back over the good and the bad,
We're aware of the number of
    good things we've had,
And in counting our blessings,
    we find when we're through
We've no reason at all to complain or be blue. . .
So thank God for the good things
    He has already done,
And be grateful to Him
    for the battles you've won,

And know that the same God
   who helped you before
Is ready and willing to help you once more,
Then with faith in your heart,
   reach out for God's hand
And accept what He sends,
   though you can't understand...
For our Father in heaven
   always knows what is best,
And if you trust His wisdom,
   your life will be blessed...
For always remember that whatever betide you,
You are never alone, for God is beside you.

—HSR

God Bless You and Keep You in His Care

There are many things in life
  we cannot understand,
But we must trust God's judgment
  and be guided by His hand. . .
And all who have God's blessing
  can rest safely in His care,
For He promises safe passage
  on the wings of faith and prayer.

—HSR

Blessing Others

In the Bible, there are many examples of fathers blessing their children. We even read that parents brought their children to Jesus so that He could place His hands on them and speak a blessing.

What a wonderful thing it is to bless another person, to ask that all of God's goodness would come into that person's life. Those words of encouragement are important. However, Jesus also taught that we must bless others not only with our words but also with our actions. What good does it do to speak a blessing over someone who is hungry if you do not give that person something to eat? Why speak a blessing over someone who is lonely, unless you are willing to provide companionship?

When God blesses, He does so in word and in deed. Ask Him this morning who He would want you to bless, then go forth to fully bless.

Make Your Day Bright
by Thinking Right and
Your Life Will Be Blessed
if You Look for the Best

Don't start your day by supposin'
   that trouble is just ahead,
It's better to stop supposin'
   and start with a prayer instead. . .
And make it a prayer of thanksgiving for the
   wonderful things God has wrought,
Like the beautiful sunrise and sunset,
   God's gifts that are free and not bought. . .
For what is the use of supposin'
   that dire things could happen to you,
Worrying about some misfortune
   that seldom if ever comes true. . .

But instead of just idle supposin',
   step forward to meet each new day
Secure in the knowledge God's near you
   to lead you each step of the way. . .
For supposin' the worst things will happen
   only helps to make them come true,
And you darken the bright, happy moments
   that the dear Lord has given to you. . .
So if you desire to be happy and get rid of
   the misery of dread,
Just give up supposin' the worst things
   and look for the best things instead.

                                    —HSR

Make Me a Channel of Blessing Today

Make me a channel of blessing today,
 I ask again and again when I pray.
Do I turn a deaf ear to the Master's
 voice or refuse to hear His direction
 and choice?
I only know at the end of the day
 that I did so little to pay my way.

—HSR

Endurance

So do not throw away your confidence; it will be richly rewarded. You need to persevere so that when you have done the will of God, you will receive what he has promised.

HEBREWS 10:35-36 NIV

The Runner

A young man runs along the street as onlookers cheer. Even though he's limping and his face reflects the pain in his injured ankle, he pushes on. Finally he finishes the course. His time is poor, but he's a winner—because he refused to give up.

Every day, life gives us reasons to give up, a full menu of disappointments, failures, and losses. And yet there is much to be gained by staying on your feet and staying in the race. No matter what you have to overcome or how long it takes you to get to the finish line, finishing means winning.

Don't give up! Ask God to strengthen you for the day ahead. And remember you don't run your race alone. God is there with you every step of the way. Even if everyone else calls it a day and heads home, He will continue to encourage you to keep going until you have the win.

God's Stairway

Step by step we climb day by day
Closer to God with each prayer we pray,
For the cry of the heart offered in prayer
Becomes just another spiritual stair
In the heavenly place where we live anew. . .
So never give up, for it's worth the climb
To live forever in endless time
Where the soul of man is safe and free
To live and love through eternity.

—HSR

My Prayer

Bless me, heavenly Father,
  forgive my erring ways.
Grant me strength to serve Thee;
  put purpose in my days.
Give me understanding,
  enough to make me kind
So I may judge all people with my heart
  and not my mind.
Teach me to be patient in everything I do,
Content to trust your wisdom
  and to follow after You.
Help me when I falter and hear me when I pray,
And receive me in Thy kingdom
  to dwell with Thee someday.

—HSR

Daily Prayers Are
Heaven's Stairs

The stairway rises heaven-high,
   the steps are dark and steep.
In weariness we climb them
   as we stumble, fall, and weep. . .
And many times we falter
   along the path of prayer,
Wondering if You hear us and if You really care.
Oh, give us some assurance;
   restore our faith anew,
So we can keep on climbing
   the stairs of prayer to You. . .
For we are weak and wavering,
   uncertain and unsure,
And only meeting You in prayer
   can help us to endure
All life's trials and troubles,
   its sickness, pain, and sorrow
And give us strength and courage
   to face and meet tomorrow.

—HSR

The Willow

A row of weeping willow trees leans with the wind that's blowing off the lake. Their branches whip and lash out to one side. Thin wisps of leaves spiral out and flutter in the cold air. The willow grows well in cold, windy places because its roots go deep and hold tight. It bends, but it does not break.

Every day we face the winds of life—a struggling economy, unexpected setbacks, illness, to name just a few. We can take the beating and hope for the best, or we can become willow trees by allowing our roots to go down deep into God.

As you spend time with Him each morning, He will show you how to bend without breaking, how to sway without snapping in two. He will teach you how to survive adversity by calling on your inner strength—courage, faith, and endurance.

With God All Things Are Possible

Nothing is ever too hard to do
If your faith is strong and your
purpose is true. . .
So never give up, and never stop—
Just journey on to the mountaintop!

—HSR

This Too Will Pass Away

If I can endure for this minute
   whatever is happening to me
No matter how heavy my heart is
   or how dark the moment might be—
If I can remain calm and quiet
   with all my world crashing about me,
Secure in the knowledge God loves me
   when everyone else seems to doubt me—
If I can but keep on believing
   what I know in my heart to be true,
That darkness will fade with the morning
   and that this will pass away, too—
Then nothing in life can defeat me,
   for as long as this knowledge remains,
I can suffer whatever is happening,
   for I know God will break all the chains
That are binding me tight in the darkness
   and trying to fill me with fear. . .
For there is no night without dawning,
   and I know that my morning is near.

—HSR

A Prayer for Patience

God, teach me to be patient,
   teach me to go slow—
Teach me how to wait on You
   when my way I do not know.
Teach me sweet forbearance
   when things do not go right
So I remain unruffled when others grow uptight.
Teach me how to quiet my racing, rising heart
So I might hear the answer
   You are trying to impart.
Teach me to let go, dear God,
   and pray undisturbed until
My heart is filled with inner peace
   and I learn to know Your will.

—HSR

Without faith it is impossible to please God, because anyone who comes to him must believe that he exists and that he rewards those who earnestly seek him.

HEBREWS 11:6 NIV

Faith That Pleases God

Out of sight, out of mind. That's what we say about infants. They don't have the capacity to care about what they can't see. But as they grow, they begin more and more to recognize and acknowledge the voice of a parent over the phone, the wind in the trees, seeds germinating below the soil, and other of life's unseen realities.

Faith is the acknowledgement that God is present even though we can't see Him. He is pleased when we begin to reach out to Him, acknowledge Him, see Him with the eyes of our hearts. It means we're growing, maturing, preparing to take hold of the powerful, spiritual, unseen forces all around us.

Are you ready, this morning, to begin your life of faith? God has an unlimited supply of wonders He's been waiting to show you.

Trust God

Take heart and meet each minute
   with faith in God's great love,
Aware that every day of life
   is controlled by God above. . .
And never dread tomorrow
   or what the future brings—
Just pray for strength and courage
   and trust God in all things.

—HSR

Finding Faith in a Flower

Sometimes when faith is running low
And I cannot fathom why things are so,
I walk among the flowers that grow
And learn the answers to all I would know...
For among my flowers I have come to see
Life's miracle and its mystery,
And standing in silence and reverie,
My faith comes flooding back to me.

—HSR

Climb Till Your
Dream Comes True

Often your tasks will be many,
  and more than you think you can do.
Often the road will be rugged,
  and the hills insurmountable, too.
But always remember, the hills ahead
  are never as steep as they seem,
And with faith in your heart, start upward
  and climb till you reach your dream.
For nothing in life that is worthy
  is ever too hard to achieve
If you have the courage to try it
  and you have the faith to believe.
For faith is a force that is greater
  than knowledge or power or skill,
And many defeats turn to triumphs
  if you trust in God's wisdom and will.
For faith is a mover of mountains—
  there's nothing that God cannot do—
So start out today with faith in your heart
  and climb till your dream comes true.

—HSR

Faith in Troubled Times

What a world we live in—even the tedium of our everyday lives is marked with danger. It would be easy to give in to fear and give up on living. But we don't, because God has given us a gift that shines brightly even in the darkness. He has given us—faith!

Faith is a simple concept, really. It is an inner confidence that God is in control of all things, that He honors the promises in His book, the Bible, and that He will never forsake us. He is present and a wellspring of strength, wisdom, and peace when we feel powerless and afraid. Yes, we are all human beings. We struggle, but we hold on to our faith.

What are you dealing with this morning? Nagging worry, an unresolved argument, failure (real or imagined)? Trust Him with every plan for the day ahead. Give it all to Him. He's listening.

Your Life Will Be Blessed If You Look for the Best

It's easy to grow downhearted
  when nothing goes your way,
It's easy to be discouraged
  when you have a troublesome day,
But trouble is only a challenge
  to spur you on to achieve
The best that God has to offer,
  if you have the faith to believe!

—HSR

God's Waiting to Share

When you're troubled and worried
   and sick at heart
And your plans are upset
   and your world falls apart,
Remember God's ready and waiting to share
The burden you find too heavy to bear. . .
So with faith, let go and let God lead the way
Into a brighter and less-troubled day.
For God has a plan for everyone,
If we learn to pray, "Thy will be done."
For nothing in life is without God's design
For each life is fashioned by the hand
   that's divine.

—HSR

Somebody Loves You

Somebody loves you more than you know,
Somebody goes with you wherever you go,
Somebody really and truly cares
And lovingly listens to all of your prayers. . .
Don't doubt for a minute that this is not true,
For God loves His children
    and takes care of them, too. . .
And all of His treasures are yours to share
If you love Him completely
    and show that you care. . .
And if you walk in His footsteps
    and have faith to believe,
There's nothing you ask for
    that you will not receive!

—HSR

I will sing of your might;
I will sing aloud of your
steadfast love in the morning.
For you have been a fortress
for me and a refuge
in the day of my distress.

PSALM 59:16 NRSV

Incomparable Love

*D*o we really believe the God who created us, loves us? Most of us would say we do—but do we really?

Looking at it rationally, there doesn't seem to be much reason for God to love us. Blessed with a free will, we've pretty much made a mess of things. And yet, it doesn't seem to matter. He knew we would, and before we drew our first breaths, He had already made a way around our messes, filling up the deficit with His own unimaginable sacrifice. In the end, we know God loves us, because He says so and because He proved it.

As you meet with God this morning, don't waste time wondering if God loves you—He does. Instead, bless Him by soaking up His love, letting it wash over you and make you whole. Don't try to understand why God loves you, just receive it with thanksgiving.

What Is Love?

What is love? No words can define it—
It's something so great only God could design it.
Wonder of wonders, beyond man's conception—
And only in God can love find true perfection. . .
For love means much more
    than small words can express,
For what man calls love is so very much less
Than the beauty and depth
    and the true richness of
God's gift to mankind of compassion from above
For love has become a word that's misused,
Perverted, distorted, and often abused

To speak of light romance or some affinity for,
A passing attraction that is seldom much more
Than a mere interlude of inflamed fascination,
A romantic fling of no lasting duration. . .
But love is enduring and patient and kind—
It judges all with the heart, not with the mind. . .
And love can transform the most commonplace
Into beauty and splendor
   and sweetness and grace. . .
For love is unselfish, giving more than it takes—
And no matter what happens,
   love never forsakes.
It's faithful and trusting and always believing,
Guileless and honest and never deceiving.
Yes, love is beyond what man can define,
For love is immortal and God's gift is divine!

                            —HSR

God's Love

God's love is like an island
   in life's ocean vast and wide—
A peaceful, quiet shelter
   from the restless, rising tide.
God's love is like an anchor
   when the angry billows roll—
A mooring in the storms of life,
   a stronghold for the soul.
God's love is like a fortress,
   and we seek protection there
When the waves of tribulation
   seem to drown us in despair.
God's love is like a harbor
   where our souls can find sweet rest
From the struggle and the tension
   of life's fast and futile quest.
God's love is like a beacon
   burning bright with faith and prayer,
And through the changing scenes of life,
   we can find a haven there.

—HSR

Beyond Human Love

What a mess we make sometimes trying to love one another! Even though we have the best intentions, we often fail because we do not have an accurate idea of what real love is.

The Bible tells us that love as God intended it is faithful and constant, patient and kind, forgiving and cleansing. It is humble, generous, and unselfish. To love as God loves is to seek another's benefit over our own, being faithful in commitment despite the temptation to give up.

If we really desire to love as God loves, we must first surrender our heart and will to Him, giving Him free reign over our thoughts, actions, and emotions. Love born of selfish desires and wrong motives will not thrive. It will always seek our good rather than that of the other person.

This morning, let God transform your love for others. Imagine how things would change if we all loved as God loves.

The House of Prayer

Just close your eyes and open your heart
And feel your cares and worries depart.
Just yield yourself to the Father above
And let Him hold you secure in His love. . .
For life on earth grows more involved
With endless problems that can't be solved,
But God only asks us to do our best,
Then He will take over and finish the rest. . .
So when you are tired, discouraged, and blue,
There's always one door that is opened to you
And that is the door to the house of prayer,

And you'll find God waiting to meet you there...
And the house of prayer is no farther away
Than the quiet spot where you kneel and pray.
For the heart is a temple when God is there
As we place ourselves in His loving care...
And He hears every prayer and answers each one
When we pray in His name, "Thy will be done."
And the burdens that seemed too heavy to bear
Are lifted away on the wings of prayer.

—HSR

On the Wings of Prayer

On the wings of prayer
   our burdens take flight
And our load of care
   becomes bearably light
And our heavy hearts are lifted above
To be healed by the balm
   of God's wonderful love. . .
And the tears in our eyes
   are dried by the hands
Of a loving Father who understands
All of our problems,
   our fears and despair
When we take them to Him
   on the wings of prayer.

—HSR

Surrender

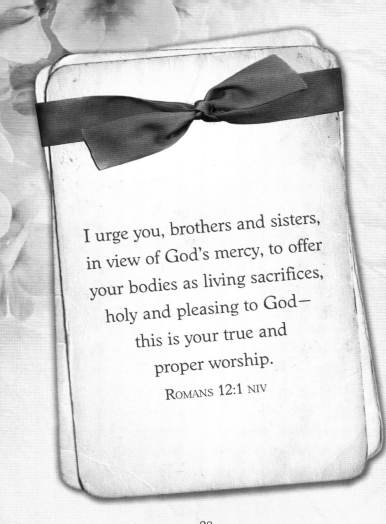

I urge you, brothers and sisters, in view of God's mercy, to offer your bodies as living sacrifices, holy and pleasing to God— this is your true and proper worship.

ROMANS 12:1 NIV

Living Sacrifices

A curious word—*sacrifice*. We tend to think of it only in the context of giving something up. But true sacrifice is two-sided. It implies that as one thing is surrendered, another gains life. We see it as we remove new growth from a branch in order to fortify the whole tree, as we redirect vacation funds to a charity in need, or set aside plans for a new car in order to pay for a son or daughter's year at college.

All of these are virtuous, but God has called us to an even higher level of sacrifice. He asks that we surrender ourselves and all that we are for His higher purposes.

Are you willing, this morning, to give God all your plans and dreams, talents and gifts—for the richer, fuller use He can make of them? He has promised to transform your sacrifice into great reward for you and for others.

More of Thee—Less of Me

Take me and break me and make me, dear God,
   just what You want me to be.
Give me the strength to accept what You send
   and eyes with the vision to see
All the small, arrogant ways that I have
   and the vain little things that I do.
Make me aware that I'm often concerned more
   with myself than with You.
Uncover before me my weakness and greed
   and help me to search deep inside
So I may discover how easy it is
   to be selfishly lost in my pride. . .
And then in Thy goodness and mercy,
   look down on this weak, erring one
And tell me that I am forgiven
   for all I've so willfully done,
And teach me to humbly start following
   the path that the dear Savior trod
So I'll find at the end of life's journey
   a home in the city of God.

—HSR

Show Me More Clearly the Way to Serve and Love You More Each Day

God, help me in my feeble way
To somehow do something each day
To show You that I love You best
And that my faith will stand each test,
And let me serve You every day
And feel You near me when I pray.
Oh, hear my prayer, dear God above,
And make me worthy of Your love.

—HSR

Let Not Your Heart Be Troubled

Whenever I am troubled and lost in deep despair,
I bundle all my troubles up
   and go to God in prayer. . .
I tell Him I am heartsick and lost and lonely, too,
That my mind is deeply burdened
   and I don't know what to do. . .
But I know He stilled the tempest
   and calmed the angry sea,
And I humbly ask if, in His love,
   He'll do the same for me. . .
And then I just keep quiet
   and think only thoughts of peace,
And if I abide in stillness
   my restless murmurings cease.

—HSR

The Seed that Dies

A seed may be full of potential but has no purpose until it's placed in the ground where soil and rain go to work on it. Only then can that seed become what God intended, a plant producing flower and fruit—and future seed!

In a similar way, our lives lack direction until surrendered to God. The decision to plant ourselves in Him is a death of sorts, in that it is the death of our plans and dreams. But it also includes a birth of great promise in that it frees God to fulfill all the purposes He has for us. Gifts and talents given over to His control come to full bloom in ways we could never have imagined!

Is there something you need to surrender to God this morning? When you put your trust in Him, you'll be amazed at how your life will blossom with purpose and fulfillment!

Now I Lay Me Down to Sleep

I remember so well this prayer I said
Each night as my mother tucked me in bed,
And today this same prayer is still the best way
To sign off with God at the end of the day
And to ask Him your soul to safely keep
As you wearily close your tired eyes in sleep,
Feeling content that the Father above
Will hold you secure in His great arms of love...

And having His promise that if ere you wake
His angels reach down, your sweet soul to take
Is perfect assurance that, awake or asleep,
God is always right there to tenderly keep
All of His children ever safe in His care,
For God's here and He's there
    and He's everywhere. . .
So into His hands each night as I sleep
I commend my soul for the dear Lord to keep,
Knowing that if my soul should take flight
It will soar to the land where there is no night.
                                    —HSR

Let Your Wish
Become a Prayer

Put your dearest wish
  in God's hands today
And discuss it with Him
  as you faithfully pray,
And you can be sure
  your wish will come true
If God feels your wish
  will be good for you...
There's no problem too big
  and no question too small,
Just ask God in faith
  and He'll answer them all—
Not always at once,
  so be patient and wait,
For God never comes
  too soon or too late...
So trust in His wisdom
  and believe in His word,
For no prayer's unanswered
  and no prayer's unheard.

—HSR

You turned my wailing into
dancing; you removed my
sackcloth and clothed me
with joy, that my heart
may sing your praises
and not be silent.
LORD my God,
I will praise you forever.

PSALM 30:11-12 NIV

Running After Happiness

Our society seems preoccupied with having a good time, rustling up all the happiness we possibly can. But somehow it isn't working. Look around and you will see sadness, discouragement, and disappointment everywhere. Maybe happiness, a fleeting emotion at best, isn't what we are really looking for.

The Bible has precious little to say about happiness. Instead it talks about joy. You might think the two are synonymous, but they aren't. The primary difference is that happiness comes and goes, but joy sticks around. Since it is a God quality, joy is as constant as God Himself.

Don't bother running after happiness. Instead, let your heart rejoice in the things you are learning from God as you meet with Him each morning. The joy that comes from knowing Him will be there when the hard times come and you need it most.

God Is Always There to Hear Our Smallest Prayer

Let us find joy in the news of His birth,
And let us find comfort
   and strength for each day
In knowing that Christ walked
   this same earthly way,
So He knows all our needs
   and He hears every prayer,
And He keeps all His children
   always safe in His care. . .

And whenever we're troubled and lost in despair,
We have but to seek Him and ask Him in prayer
To guide and direct us and help us to bear
Our sickness and sorrow, our worry and care. . .
So once more at Christmas
    let the whole world rejoice
In the knowledge He answers
    every prayer that we voice.

—HSR

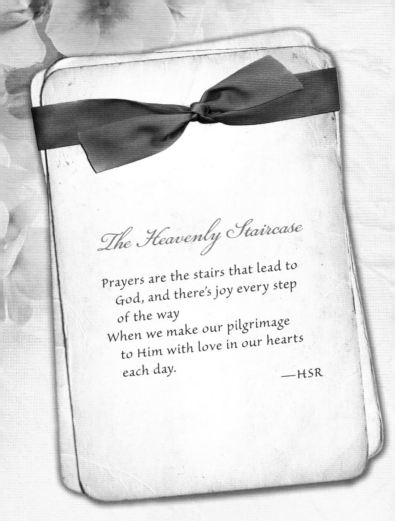

The Heavenly Staircase

Prayers are the stairs that lead to
  God, and there's joy every step
  of the way
When we make our pilgrimage
  to Him with love in our hearts
  each day.

—HSR

Rejoice in All Things

The Bible instructs us to rejoice—especially in trying times. Does that seem curious to you? Why would God ask us to rejoice when bad things happen? The answer lies both in our human nature and in God's greatness.

When trouble strikes, the natural human response is to cry out for help. And when we do, God is waiting. He doesn't bring trouble to our lives. Most often we bring it on ourselves. But He is there to help whenever we need Him. In this way, our troubles become opportunities to connect with our heavenly Father. That's truly something to rejoice about.

When you encounter troubling times, don't despair. Instead rejoice, for you have a loving, benevolent God who is committed to helping you. His help may not be what you expect, but it will always be exactly what you need.

A Sure Way to a Happy Day

Happiness is something we create in our mind,
It's not something you search for
   and so seldom find.
It's just waking up and beginning the day
By counting our blessings and kneeling to pray.
It's giving up thoughts that breed discontent
And accepting what comes as a gift heaven-sent.

It's giving up wishing for things we have not
And making the best of whatever we've got.
It's knowing that life is determined for us
And pursuing our tasks
    without fret, fume, or fuss. . .
For it's by completing what God gives us to do
That we find real contentment
    and happiness, too.

—HSR

In God's Tomorrow
There Is Eternal Spring

All nature heeds the call of spring
  as God awakens everything,
And all that seemed so dead and still
  experiences a sudden thrill
As springtime lays a magic hand
  across God's vast and fertile land.
Oh, the joy in standing by
  to watch a sapphire springtime sky
Or see a fragile flower break through
  what just a day ago or two
Seemed barren ground still hard with frost,
  for in God's world, no life is lost,
And flowers sleep beneath the ground,
  but when they hear spring's waking sound,
They push themselves through layers of clay
  to reach the sunlight of God's day.
And man and woman, like flowers, too, must sleep
  until called from the darkened deep
To live in that place where angels sing
  and where there is eternal spring.

—HSR

How rich is God's grace,
which he has given to us
so fully and freely.

EPHESIANS 1:7-8 NCV

The Riches of His Grace

Do you consider yourself a wealthy person? That may depend on how you define wealth. Most people would say, especially toward the end of their lives, that true wealth has little to do with money and possessions. True riches are those things money can't buy.

The Bible defines wealth as the pouring out of God's grace in our lives. And what is grace? It is the sum of those many unearned, undeserved benefits that come from relationship with God. It includes but is not limited to His forgiveness, His love, His provision, His healing, His presence, His wisdom and counsel, His guidance—the list is truly limitless.

This very morning, you can become a wealthy person by trading your regret and hopelessness for joy, forgiveness, and endless possibilities. Why live in poverty when you can enjoy the riches God has provided? Become truly wealthy by stepping up to receive God's grace.

God Will Not Fail You

When life seems empty
   and there's no place to go,
When your heart is troubled
   and your spirits are low,
When friends seem few and nobody cares,
There is always God to hear your prayers. . .
And whatever you're facing will seem much less
When you go to God and confide and confess,
For the burden that seems too heavy to bear
God lifts away on the wings of prayer. . .

And seen through God's eyes
    earthly troubles diminish
And we're given new strength
    to face and to finish
Life's daily tasks as they come along
If we pray for strength to keep us strong. . .
So go to our Father when troubles assail you,
For His grace is sufficient
    and He'll never fail you.

—HSR

My Daily Prayer

God, be my resting place and my protection
In hours of trouble, defeat, and dejection—
May I never give away to self-pity and sorrow,
May I always be sure of a better tomorrow,
May I stand undaunted come what may,
Secure in the knowledge I have only to pray
And ask my Creator and Father above
To keep me serene in His grace and His love.

—HSR

Extravagant Grace

*H*ave you ever asked yourself, "What can I do to make God love me? What can I do to get Him to bless me?" Most of us have asked those questions. But it isn't easy to embrace the answer. There is nothing we can do to earn God's love or to convince Him to bless us. He just does! We call it "grace."

Grace is God's undeserved favor—His gift! Imagine that someone gave you a lavish gift and you insisted on paying for it. Wouldn't that be inappropriate, even insulting?

Receive God's gift of extravagant grace this morning. Open your heart wide, and freely take of His love, His forgiveness, His joy, His comfort—all that He has to offer. You could never make God love you or bless you. His love can't be bought at any price. Instead, He gives His love away and asks only for your thanks.

God Is Never Beyond Our Reach

No one ever sought the Father
   and found He was not there,
And no burden is too heavy
   to be lightened by a prayer.
No problem is too intricate,
   and no sorrow that we face
Is too deep and devastating
   to be softened by His grace.
No trials and tribulations
   are beyond what we can bear
If we share them with our Father
   as we talk to Him in prayer. . .

And men of every color, every race,
    and every creed
Have but to seek the Father
    in their deepest hour of need.
God asks for no credentials—
    He accepts us with our flaws.
He is kind and understanding
    and He welcomes us because
We are His erring children
    and He loves us, every one,
And He freely and completely forgives
    all that we have done,
Asking only if we're ready to follow
    where He leads,
Content that in His wisdom
    He will answer all our needs.

—HSR

No Favor Do I Seek Today

I come not to ask, to plead,
   or implore You—
I just come to tell You
   how much I adore You.
For to kneel in Your presence
   makes me feel blessed,
For I know that You know
   all my needs best,
And it fills me with joy
   just to linger with you,
As my soul You replenish
   and my heart You renew.
For prayer is much more than
   just asking for things—
It's the peace and contentment
   that quietness brings.
So thank You again for
   Your mercy and love
And for making me heir
   to Your kingdom above.

—HSR

Reaching
Out to Others

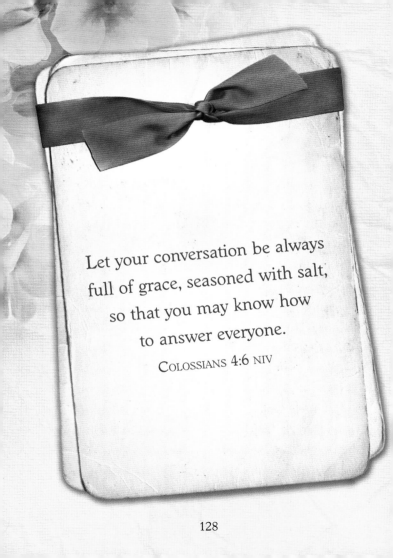

Let your conversation be always
full of grace, seasoned with salt,
so that you may know how
to answer everyone.

COLOSSIANS 4:6 NIV

A Risk Worth Taking

Do you shy away from people who need help? Maybe you fear they will try to take advantage of you. Or you may believe you don't have much to offer. You're right to think that reaching out to others can be risky. The moment you start to care about someone, to really listen, you become vulnerable. You risk the real possibility of exploitation and rejection.

And yet, the Bible tells us that helping, encouraging, listening, praying for others is something God wants us to do. That takes courage and humility and a heart that is quick to listen and obey when God speaks.

You can't help everyone. There are just too many needs and too many needy people. But you can ask God to show you the people He wants you to reach out to today, those He has given you the resources to help. Those encounters are well worth the risk.

Not to Seek, Lord, But to Share

Dear God, much too often
   we seek You in prayer
Because we are wallowing
   in our own self-despair.
We make every word we lamentingly speak
An imperative plea for whatever we seek.
We pray for ourselves
   and so seldom for others—
We're concerned with our problems
   and not with our brothers.
We seem to forget, Lord,
   that the sweet hour of prayer

Is not for self-seeking but to place in Your care
All the lost souls, unloved and unknown,
And to keep praying for them
    until they're your own.
For it's never enough to seek God in prayer
With no thought of others
    who are lost in despair.
So teach us, dear God, that the power of prayer
Is made stronger by placing
    the world in Your care.

—HSR

I Think of You and I Pray for You, Too

Often during a busy day
I pause for a minute to silently pray,
I mention the names of those I love
And treasured friends I am fondest of,
For it doesn't matter where we pray
If we honestly mean the words we say,
For God is always listening to hear
The prayers that are made by a heart
that's sincere.

—HSR

A Little Goodness

God is good to us—abundantly, consistently, unfailingly good. And all He asks in return is that we are good to one another. You can do that by simply giving what you have—a friendly smile, a word of encouragement, a loving act, a word of blessing, a gesture of thanks—to those who need it. When you reach out to others, you are acting like your heavenly Father, learning His ways.

But what if the person who needs a little goodness this morning is you? That's all right. You can't give what you don't have. Reach out to God first, for He is the only one who can mend your hurting heart. Then reach out to those who profess their love for God. Let Him show you His goodness through them.

God has so much He wants to give you, so much He wants to do in and through your life. Reach out for His goodness.

Widen My Vision

God, open my eyes so I may see
And feel Your presence close to me.
Give me strength for my stumbling feet
As I battle the crowd on life's busy street,
And widen the vision of my unseeing eyes
So in passing faces I'll recognize

Not just a stranger, unloved and unknown,
But a friend with a heart
    that is much like my own.
Give me perception to make me aware
That scattered profusely on life's thoroughfare
Are the best gifts of God that we daily pass by
As we look at the world with an unseeing eye.

—HSR

The Power of Prayer

I am only a worker employed
  by the Lord,
And great is my gladness
  and rich my reward
If I can just spread the wonderful story
That God is the answer
  to eternal glory. . .
And only the people
  who read my poems
Can help me to reach
  more hearts and homes,
Bringing new hope and
  comfort and cheer
Telling sad hearts
  there is nothing to fear,
And what greater joy
  could there be than to share
The love of God
  and the power of prayer.

—HSR

Teach me to do your will,
for you are my God.
Let your good spirit
lead me on a level path.

PSALM 143:10 NRSV

A Special Purpose

What is the meaning of my life? People have been asking that question as long as human beings have walked on the earth. Sure, we stay busy, take care of business, but deep down inside we know that there must be something more.

The Bible says that God has a purpose for every one of us—a special, unique plan for every life. Looking around at the masses of humankind, you may wonder how this could be true. But God doesn't ask us to determine His intention for every life, just our own.

This morning, ask Him to reveal His purpose for you. It won't come all at once. But as you open your heart, you will sense His tender hand leading you, helping you glimpse what He has in store for you. Baby steps at first and then bigger steps as you march confidently into His perfect will.

Thy Will Be Done

God did not promise sun without rain,
Light without darkness or joy without pain.
He only promised strength for the day
When the darkness comes
   and we lose our way. . .
For only through sorrow do we grow more aware
That God is our refuge in times of despair,
For when we are happy and life's bright and fair,
We often forget to kneel down in prayer. . .
But God seems much closer
   and needed much more

When trouble and sorrow
   stand outside our door,
For then we seek shelter in His wondrous love,
And we ask Him to send us help from above. . .
And that is the reason we know it is true
That bright, shining hours
   and dark, sad ones, too,
Are part of the plan God made for each one,
And all we can pray is "Thy will be done."
And know that you are never alone
For God is your Father
   and you're one of His own.

—HSR

Put Your Problems in God's Hands for He Completely Understands

Although it sometimes seems to us
  our prayers have not been heard,
God always knows our every need
  without a single word,
And He will not forsake us
  even though the way is steep,
For always He is near to us,
  a tender watch to keep. . .
And in good time He will answer us,
  and in His love He'll send
Greater things than we have asked
  and blessings without end. . .
So though we do not understand
  why trouble comes to man,
Can we not be contented
  just to know it is God's plan?

—HSR

Close to Home

*D*id you know that some people are afraid to find out what God's will is for them? They imagine that God might ask them to uproot their lives or take on some mission far too difficult for them. Sure, God's will does cause some people to make great sacrifices, travel to faraway places, and do things they never imagined doing. But for most of us, God's will hits close to home.

For example, God's will most often involves talents we already know we possess, in places where we already reside. If you're wondering about God's will for your life, you might even find that you are already doing it. God places His will inside us before we are ever born. For that reason, even if He calls you to a faraway place, it will be one you have always wondered about, longed to see.

Life isn't random. It's been planned in great detail. Ask God to reveal His plan for you.

Not What You Want,
but What God Wills

Do you want what you want when you want it,
   do you pray and expect a reply?
And when it's not instantly answered,
   do you feel that God passed you by?
Well, prayers that are prayed in this manner
   are really not prayers at all,
For you can't go to God in a hurry
   and expect Him to answer your call.
For prayers are not meant for obtaining
   what we selfishly wish to acquire,
For God in His wisdom refuses the things
   that we wrongly desire. . .
And don't pray for freedom from trouble
   or pray that life's trials pass you by.

Instead pray for strength and for courage
    to meet life's dark hours and not cry
That God was not there when you called Him
    and He turned a deaf ear to your prayer
And just when you need Him most of all
    He left you alone in despair.
Wake up! You are missing completely
    the reason and purpose of prayer,
Which is really to keep us contented
    that God holds us safe in His care. . .
And God only answers our pleadings
    when He knows that our wants fill a need,
And whenever our will becomes His will,
    there is no prayer that God does not heed.

                            —HSR

Prayers Can't Be Answered
Until They Are Prayed

Life without purpose is barren indeed,
There can't be a harvest
    unless you plant seed.
Games can't be won
    unless they are played,
And prayers can't be answered
    unless they are prayed...
So whatever is wrong
    with your life today,
You'll find a solution
    if you kneel down and pray
Pray for a purpose to make
    life worth living,
And pray for the joy of unselfish giving...
For great is your gladness
    and rich your reward
When you make your life's purpose
    the choice of the Lord.

—HSR

God's Presence

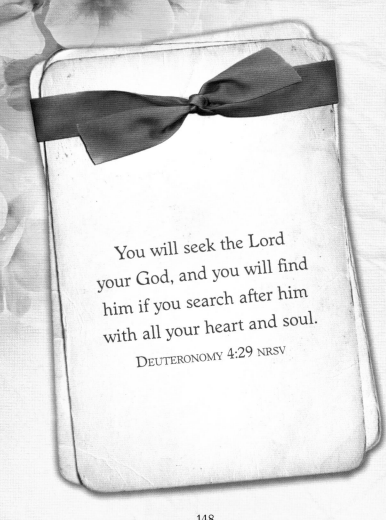

You will seek the Lord
your God, and you will find
him if you search after him
with all your heart and soul.

DEUTERONOMY 4:29 NRSV

In His Presence

Close your eyes. Now try to imagine what it would be like to be in God's presence. He's a king, so He would be on a throne, right? Would you be able to walk right in or would He be heavily guarded? And how would you feel? Frightened, awed, humbled, nervous?

There is only one thing *more* amazing than the awesome greatness of our Almighty God, Creator of heaven and earth. That one thing is the way He cares for us. He has given us open access, invited us to come into His presence. What an amazing privilege and one we should never take lightly.

As you come before God each morning, remember to thank Him for loving you and making a way for you to come into His holy presence. Ask Him to cleanse your heart and make you worthy of the honor.

I Come to Meet You

I come to meet You, God, and as I linger here
I seem to feel You very near.
A rustling leaf, a rolling slope
Speak to my heart of endless hope.
The sun just rising in the sky,
The waking birdlings as they fly,
The grass all wet with morning dew
Are telling me I just met You. . .

And gently thus the day is born
As night gives way to breaking morn,
And once again I've met You, God,
And worshipped on Your holy sod. . .
For who could see the dawn break through
Without a glimpse of heaven and You?
For who but God could make the day
And softly put the night away?

—HSR

The Mystery of Prayer

Beyond that which words can interpret
   or theology explain,
The soul feels a shower of refreshment
   that falls like the gentle rain
On hearts that are parched with problems
   and are searching to find the way
To somehow attract God's attention
   through well-chosen words as they pray,
Not knowing that God in His wisdom
   can sense all man's worry and woe,
For there is nothing man can conceal
   that God does not already know. . .
So kneel in prayer in His presence
   and you'll find no need to speak,
For softly in quiet communion,
   God grants you the peace that you seek.

—HSR

Miracle and Mystery

Have you ever heard the term "God-shaped hole?" It's that hollow, hurting place in each of us that can never be filled by anything or anyone other than God Himself. He designed us that way, because He knows we need Him at the very center of our lives.

In the Bible God calls our bodies temples of His Holy Spirit. That means that when we invite Him in, His Spirit actually takes up residence within us. Because of that, He is always with us, as close as our breath. Wherever we are, He is there, and He promises never to leave.

Thank God this morning for filling the God-shaped hole in your heart. Thank Him for promising to be with you always. And then ask Him to make you a worthy temple for His presence, cleansing you of all sinfulness and rebellion. It's both a miracle and a mystery.

Anywhere Is a Place of Prayer
If God Is There

I have prayed on my knees in the morning,
  I have prayed as I walked along,
I have prayed in the silence and darkness,
  and I've prayed to the tune of a song.
I have prayed in the midst of a triumph,
  and I've prayed when I suffered defeat,
I have prayed on the sands of the seashore
  where the waves of the ocean beat.
I have prayed in a velvet, hushed forest
  where the quietness calmed my fears,
I have prayed through suffering and heartache
  when my eyes were blinded with tears.

I have prayed in churches and chapels,
   cathedrals and synagogues, too,
But often I had the feeling
   that my prayers were not getting through. . .
And I realized then that our Father
   is not really concerned when we pray
Or impressed by our manner of worship
   or the eloquent words that we say.
He is only concerned with our feelings,
   and He looks deep into our hearts
And hears the cry of our souls' deep need
   that no words could ever impart. . .
So it isn't the prayer that's expressive
   or offered in some special spot,
That's the sincere plea of a sinner,
   and God can tell whether or not
We honestly seek His forgiveness
   and earnestly mean what we say,
And then and then only God answers
   the prayers that we fervently pray.

—HSR

What More Can You Ask?

God's love endures forever—
   what a wonderful thing to know
When the tides of life run against you
   and your spirit is downcast and low.
God's kindness is ever around you
   always ready to freely impart
Strength to your faltering spirit,
   cheer to your lonely heart.
God's presence is ever beside you,
   as near as the reach of your hand.
You have but to tell Him your troubles—
   there is nothing He won't understand. . .
And knowing God's love is unfailing,
   and His mercy unending and great,
You have but to trust in His promise,
   "God comes not too soon or too late". . .
So wait with a heart that is patient
   for the goodness of God to prevail,
For never do prayers go unanswered,
   and His mercy and love never fail.

                     —HSR

God once said, "Let the light
shine out of the darkness!"
This is the same God who
made his light shine in
our hearts by letting us
know the glory of God
that is in the face of Christ.

2 CORINTHIANS 4:6 NCV

Try to Imagine

Imagine yourself standing on a mountaintop gazing at the stars, swimming along observing the amazing world under the ocean, or looking into the face of a sleeping child. These are wonders we human beings can barely comprehend. Now think about the sun and the moon and the seasons all created for us. And what about the air we breath, the colors, tastes, and textures of life. Awesome!

Next take a moment to think about the things you cannot see! God's unfailing love and His promises to hear your prayers and intervene in the circumstances of your life. Consider His heart of forgiveness and how, once confessed, He puts your unworthy thoughts and deeds behind you, never to bring them up again.

As you meet with Him this morning, praise Him for His indescribable glory. Let your heart burst forth in worship. God loves to hear you praise Him with a grateful heart.

The Masterpiece

Framed by the vast, unlimited sky,
Bordered by mighty waters,
Sheltered by beautiful woodland groves,
Scented with flowers that bloom and die,
Protected by giant mountain peaks
The land of the great unknown
Snowcapped and towering, a nameless place
That beckons man on as the gold he seeks,

Bubbling with life and earthly joys
Reeking with pain and mortal strife
Dotted with wealth and material gains
Built on ideals of girls and boys,
Streaked with toil,
    opportunity's banner unfurled
Stands out the masterpiece of art
Painted by the one great God
A picture of the world.

—HSR

The Mystery and Miracle of His Creative Hand

In the beauty of a snowflake
   falling softly on the land
Is the mystery and the miracle
   of God's great, creative hand.
What better answers are there
   to prove His holy being
Than the wonders all around us
   that are ours just for the seeing?

—HSR

A Lofty Ambition

A famous preacher once wrote that he spends his first waking moments praying, "Today, Lord, glorify Yourself at my expense." Think about what that means. He is stating His willingness to surrender anything that fails to bring glory to His God.

That sounds pretty lofty, especially when our all-too-human hearts are crying out for what *we* want. It means letting go of our desires, our plans, and the control over every aspect of our lives. It means acting and speaking *only* in ways that please Him. Yes, it is a lofty ambition to glorify God in all we do, an ambition we can achieve only as we surrender to Him completely.

As you begin your day, ask God to glorify Himself through your words, attitudes, and actions. Ask yourself in every situation, "What can I do to glorify God in this situation?" Then do it!

Everywhere Across the Land
You See God's Face
and Touch His Hand

Each time you look up in the sky
Or watch the fluffy clouds drift by,
Or feel the sunshine, warm and bright,
Or watch the dark night turn to light,
Or hear a bluebird brightly sing,

Or see the winter turn to spring,
Or stop to pick a daffodil,
Or gather violets on some hill,
Or touch a leave or see a tree,
It's all God whispering, "This is Me...
And I am faith and I am light
And in Me there shall be no night."

—HSR

Show Me the Way

Show me the way
    not to fortune and fame
Not how to win laurels
    or praise for my name,
But show me the way
    to spread the great story
That Thine is the kingdom
    and power and glory.

—HSR

Be Glorified

*I*f you have children, you've probably had to
smile from time to time when one of your own does
something so *you*. It's in the genes, and you just have to
hope your children get the best of who you are rather
than the worst. Something very similar happens when
we allow God's Spirit to come and dwell within us.

God doesn't need to be concerned about us picking
up His negative traits because He doesn't have any.
Instead, we are infused with His goodness, His purity,
His strength, and His love. As we respond to His
presence within, we reflect His glory.

God wants to see Himself reflected in you. Imagine
the smile on His face as He sees you becoming more and
more like Him. As you meet with Him this morning, ask
Him to cleanse your heart, and then set out to be a living
expression of His glory in everything you do.

The Heavens Declare the Glory of God

You ask me how I know it's true
  that there is a living God.
A God who rules the universe—
  the sky, the sea, the sod—
A God who holds all creatures
  in the hollow of His hand,
A God who put infinity
  in one tiny grain of sand,
A God who made the seasons—
  winter, summer, fall, and spring—
And put His flawless rhythm
  into each created thing,
A God who hangs the sun out slowly
  with the break of day

And gently takes the stars in
   and puts the night away,
A God whose mighty handiwork
   defies the skill of man,
For no architect can alter
   God's perfect master plan.
What better answers are there
   to prove His holy being
Than the wonders all around us
   that are ours just for the seeing.

                 —HSR

My Garden of Prayer

My garden beautifies my yard
   and adds fragrance to the air,
But it is also my cathedral
   and my quiet place of prayer.
So little do we realize
   that the glory and the power
Of Him who made the universe
   lies hidden in a flower!

—HSR

Index

About the Author

America's beloved inspirational poet laureate, Helen Steiner Rice, has encouraged millions of people through her beautiful and uplifting verse. Born in Lorain, Ohio, in 1900, Helen was the daughter of a railroad man and an accomplished seamstress and began writing poetry at a young age.

In 1918, Helen began working for a public utilities company and eventually became one of the first female advertising managers and public speakers in the country. In January 1929, she married a wealthy banker named Franklin Rice, who later sank into depression during the Great Depression and eventually committed suicide. Helen later said that her suffering made her sensitive to the pain of others. Her sadness helped her to write some of her most uplifting verses.

Her work for a Cincinnati, Ohio, greeting card company eventually led to her nationwide popularity as a poet when her Christmas card poem "The Priceless Gift of Christmas" was first read on *The Lawrence Welk Show*. Soon Helen had produced several books of her poetry that were a source of inspiration to millions of readers.

Helen died in 1981, leaving a foundation in her name to offer assistance to the needy and the elderly. Now, more than thirty years after her death, Helen's words still speak powerfully to the hearts of readers about love and comfort, faith and hope, peace and joy.